Foreword

The Manx Kitchen is a collection of simple recipes which have been submitted by the staff, patients and volunteers of St Bridget's Hospice. Some recipes are traditionally Manx in their origination.

The book was inspired by the late Mary Edge, a regular day unit attendee, who kindly supplied St Bridget's with cakes and pastries for many months thus, seriously damaging our waistlines!

The enthusiasm shown and the quantity of recipes and tips submitted, reflects the commitment and love people hold for St Bridget's Hospice. This interest and support is truly amazing, and bears out the reputation of the Manx population's appreciation of charitable efforts.

The Manx Kitchen is the result of hard work by a group of people who want to help and make a difference. It is fitting, therefore, that the proceeds in part will contribute towards the building of a new hospice to enable the staff and volunteers of hospice to continue to assist and make a difference.

We are confident that these recipes will enhance your abilities in the kitchen and serve to widen the enjoyment your family draws from your culinary efforts.

Thank you for your support.

4	Dedication
5	Message from Mary Edge
6	Sponsors
7	Meats, Poultry & Savouries
20	Fish & Shellfish
31	Cakes
45	Breads, Bun Loaves & Puddings
60	This 'n That

DEDICATION

This book is dedicated to the late Mary Edge who, over the years, tempted and pleasured many peoples' taste buds with her delicious cakes. Throughout her life she faced extreme difficulties with her health and amazed her family and friends with her terrific strength, courage, enthusiasm and love for life and people.

Thank you, Mary, with love from all the Day Hospice Team.

ACKNOWLEDGEMENTS

The Publishers wish to thank the following people for their help with this book:

The Hospice Day Unit Team – staff, volunteers and patients
The late Margaret Whitehead   The late Paddy Lonnerghan
The late Mary Edge and family   Mary Linehan
Sue Robinson   Malcolm Penrose   Sue Matthews
Roy Blinkhorn   Bill Sneddon   Gill McBride
Jean Walters   Marjory Harper   Sarah Palmer
Hugh MacRae   Peggy Foster   Helen Makin
Jean Last   Paul Quillin   Pam Fuller
Andrew Moore   Jacquie Horne   Lyndsay Wilkinson
Cooil Bros, Bradda Martin Brunnschweiler Arthur Miller
Tracy Binnie   George Crawford   Dougie Fuller
Jo Beard   Ratcliffe's (IOM) Honey Nikki Creer
Catherine Duffy, Isle of Man College.   Moggy

The Publishers wish to express appreciation to the following who supplied photographs or illustrations:

Jan Quillin (Hospice Occupational Therapist)
Capt Stephen Carter   Harvey Briggs   Paul Parker
Colleen Corlett   Colin Slack   The Manx Experience

and some illustrations were supplied by

The Library, Manx National Heritage

St Bridget's Hospice are indebted to the following sponsors who ensured the publication of the Recipe Book:

**Manx National Farmers Union, IOM Young Farmers,
Manx Fish Producers Organisation,
Ramsey Bakery, Laxey Glen Mills, The Manx Experience.**

A Message from the late Mary Edge – the inspiration for this book - written during her later years.

Baking has played an important role in my life for over 60 years. I first started baking during the 2nd World War when I married in 1940. I have been coming to the Island all my life because of my strong Manx family connections. My maiden name was "Kelly", my father was Manx born.

When I began baking during wartime all food was rationed, so I learned very quickly how to be economical but it gave me a chance to experiment and be creative.

During this time we had to make food go a long way and also did not have the benefits of freezers. We used a box which was fixed to an outside wall and covered in a metal mesh. One positive side was houses were not centrally heated which helped us keep food for longer in the winter season.

I am used to being busy, when I ran a 14-bedroomed Bed, Breakfast and Evening Meal - up at 5 am and bed at 12 midnight.

I have baked for 63 years and during this time I have never bought a cake. Baking continues to bring me great pleasure and I still get a buzz even now when my cakes come out of the oven.

I hope that my recipes bring you the same pleasure when following them, as well as eating the finished food, as they have for me.

Mary Edge

DY ROW MAIN MIE ERRN
(a Manx wish for Good Eating)

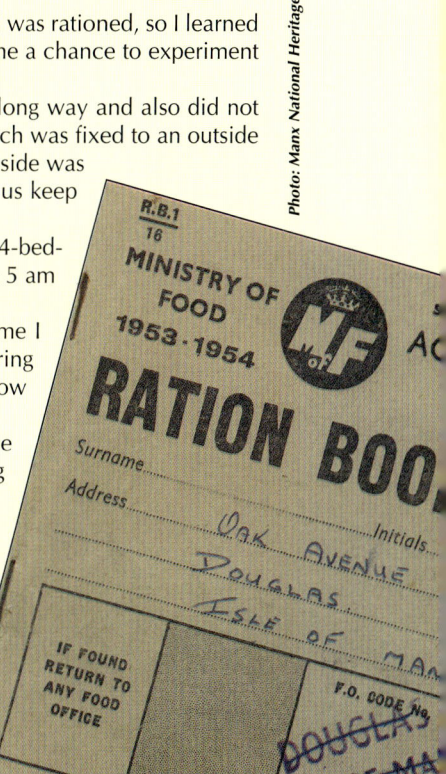

Photo: Manx National Heritage

FRESH BREAD - DELIVERED EVERY DAY

For the last 33 years, at the crack of dawn a fleet of Ramsey Bakery vans sets out to service every store in the Island, from corner shop to supermarket, with bread baked during the previous night - truly a local service. Ramsey Bakery have pleasure in supporting the production of "The Manx Kitchen" for Hospice.

RAMSEY BAKERY LIMITED
Station Road : Ramsey : Isle of Man
Telephone 01624 813624 : Fax 01624 816221

The importance of agriculture and fishing to the future of the Isle of Man has always been paramount and continues to be so to the present time.

The **Manx National Farmers Union** plays a significant part in the agricultural community through its recognition of farmers' interests and its desire to ensure that the produce of its members is recognised as being of the highest quality. Similarly, the contribution of the Island's **Young Farmers** through their expertise and their enthusiasm consolidates and assists in securing the future of the industry at a time when investment in the future is a matter of significant importance.

Manx Fish Producers Organisation Limited looks after the interests of the Island's fishermen who, though now much reduced in numbers, still ensure that locally-caught fish remains of the highest standard.

All three organisations are pleased to be associated with this book, which will assist Hospice.

LAXEY GLEN MILLS

For nearly 150 years, Laxey Glen Mills has served Island residents with the finest flour.

The Mill is proud to be associated with "The Manx Kitchen".

LAXEY GLEN MILLS LIMITED
Glen Road : Laxey : Isle of Man
Telephone 01624 861202 : Fax 01624 862278

Photo: Ian Quillin

"We are proud of the quality of Manx meat which enables us not only to serve the residents of the Isle of Man, but also to fly the Isle of Man flag on the adjacent Isle through our exports."

Malcolm Whelan, General Manager,
Isle of Man Fatstock Marketing Association.

MEATS, POULTRY & SAVOURIES

Roast Manx Lamb with Garlic

Photo: Jan Quillin

INGREDIENTS

Leg of Manx Lamb
  (ideally approx 5lb)
5 garlic cloves
Large onion
Stick of celery
Some rosemary sprigs
¾ bottle red wine
(for sauce)
1½ oz Manx butter
Carrots
Some thyme sprigs
2 tsp ground ginger
Seasoning

METHOD

Remove garlic skins and slice into quarters lengthways. Push into small holes made in lamb with a skewer along with some rosemary. Rub mixture of salt, pepper and ground ginger into skin of meat. Cover and leave for flavours to absorb for one hour.

Peel onions and carrots and, together with celery, chop into large pieces.

Melt butter in roasting tin on cooker and seal the meat quickly over a moderate heat. Remove from heat and remove meat from dish. Place vegetables in butter and meat juices and cook over moderate heat for 2-3 minutes.

Remove vegetables and place into ovenproof dish. Place meat on top, add thyme and cover.

BAKE: 425°F, Gas Mark 7, 220°C.

TIME: 30 mins, then reduce heat and pour wine over meat and

BAKE: 350°F, Gas Mark 4, 180°C.

TIME: 1½ - 1¾ hours.

Remove joint after cooking and keep warm. Strain all cooking juices and boil over moderate heat until reduced by one quarter. Thicken if needed. This dish is delicious with all fresh vegetables and especially new Manx potatoes.

Steak and Bushy's Ale pie

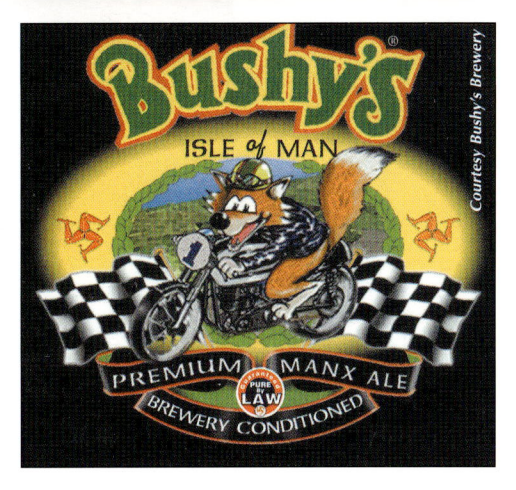

INGREDIENTS - FILLING
1½ lb Manx Steak and Kidney
Salt and Pepper to taste
¾ pint Bushy's Ale
1 tablespoon Flavo plain flour

METHOD
Mix, on a plate, flour and seasoning. Cut meat into small pieces and coat with flour. Place in a stew pan, cover with Bushy's Ale and simmer for 1 hour, stirring occasionally.

INGREDIENTS - 'RUFF PUFF' PASTRY
8 ozs Flavo plain flour
5 ozs Lard
½ teaspoon Salt
Cold water

METHOD
Mix flour and salt in a basin. Cut lard into small pieces and mix with flour, using a knife - (do not rub in lard). Mix into a stiff paste with cold water. Turn onto a floured board and roll out into a narrow strip. Fold into three, turn one of the open ends towards you and roll out again. Repeat twice more.

PIE:
Turn meat mixture into a pie dish, but do not fill more than two thirds with gravy (or the crust will be wet and sodden). If the dish is not well-filled with meat, put a pie funnel in the centre. Roll out the pastry to the shape of, but a little larger than, the top of the pie dish and cut a strip off the edge. Wet the edge of the dish and place the strip all around, moisten it and cover the pie with the remainder of the paste, pressing the edges together. Trim the edge and decorate the top with cuttings of pastry. Make a hole in the centre and brush over the surface with beaten egg or milk.

BAKE: in a hot oven - 400°-425°F, 200°-220°C, Gas Mark 6-7.

TIME: 30 minutes.

Loughtan Lamb stew with Dumplings

Photo: The Manx Experience

INGREDIENTS - STEW
2 ½ lb lean middle neck and scrag-end of Loughtan mutton or lamb
¾ lb onions (sliced)
½ lb carrots (sliced)
2 medium-sized leeks (washed and sliced)
1 large potato (peeled and sliced)
1 tbls pearl barley
2 pints hot water
2 tbls seasoned Flavo flour
salt & pepper to taste

INGREDIENTS - DUMPLINGS
4 oz self-raising flour
1 tbls fresh chopped parsley
2 oz shredded suet
salt & pepper to taste

METHOD - STEW
Cut away any excess fat from meat and dip in seasoned flour. Place large layer of meat in the bottom of a large saucepan and add some of the onions, carrots, leeks and potato plus seasoning. Add more meat and continue to layer until all ingredients are placed in saucepan. Sprinkle in the pearl barley, add hot water and bring to a simmer. Cover pan with lid and leave to simmer for approximately 2 hours.

METHOD - DUMPLINGS
Approximately 15 minutes prior to end of cooking time for stew prepare dumplings as follows:

Mix together in a bowl flour, salt, pepper and parsley. Mix in suet - do not rub in. Add sufficient water to make a stiff/elasticy dough which leaves the bowl clean. Shape into 8 dumplings.

When stew is cooked - remove the meat and vegetables with a slotted spoon. Place into warm dish, cover and keep warm. Season remaining liquid to taste and bring to a fast boil. Add dumplings, cover and cook for further 20-25 minutes making sure that boiling continues. Serve.

Crusty Chicken Casserole

INGREDIENTS

4 – 6 Manx chicken breasts
1 onion
2 shallots
1 stick celery
¼ cup water
30g butter
3 rashers Manx bacon
60g mushrooms
440g can condensed mushroom soup
300g carton sour cream
¼ cup grated Manx cheese

CHEESE BATTER INGREDIENTS

1 cup Sunrise flour
½ red pepper
½ green pepper
2 eggs
1 cup grated cheese
½ cup milk

Photo: Ian Quillin

Submitted by Marjory Harper

CHEESE BATTER METHOD

Sift flour into bowl, add diced peppers, beaten eggs, cheese and milk. Mix until just blended.

METHOD

Steam or boil chicken and roughly chop. Place chopped onion, shallots and celery in water and simmer for 15 minutes. Melt butter in pan, add chopped bacon and sliced mushrooms, cook for 3 minutes. Combine soup, sour cream, chicken and vegetables and bacon mixture. Pour into greased ovenproof dish. Spread cheese batter over the top.

BAKE: Uncovered 360°F, 185°C, Gas Mark 4.

TIME: 40 mins. Sprinkle with cheese and return to oven for 5 minutes.

MEATS, POULTRY & SAVOURIES

Top of the Stove Pot Roast

INGREDIENTS

2 large onions,
  1 stuck with cloves
4-6 tablespoons oil
3-4lb (1½- 2kg) Manx
  rump, topside or chuck
2 beef bouillon cubes
1 bay leaf
6 carrots
3 medium sliced
  potatoes
salt and pepper

METHOD

Slice the onions and trim meat of any gristle and excess fat - then tie it securely into a good shape for cooking. Heat the oil and lightly fry onions until soft. Take onions out and brown the meat very well on all sides. Put the bay leaf on top, then add onions, cloves and the bouillon cubes dissolved in 2 cups of water. Taste for seasoning, add according to taste.

Cover pot closely and cook gently over low heat.

TIME: - 2 – 2½ hours

Add the carrots and potatoes sliced for the last hour. Or cook in pressure cooker for 40-45 minutes.

Photo: Manx National Heritage

Submitted by Jean Last

Traditional Manx Broth

INGREDIENTS

4 Pints beef/chicken stock (or 3-4 stock cubes plus 4 pints water)
4 ozs Pearl barley
1½ lbs mixed vegetables (carrots, onions and turnips)
Salt and pepper to taste
(about 4 ozs of chopped cabbage may be added if desired)

METHOD:

Sweat all vegetables in small amount of butter until signs of softening are apparent. Add stock and bring to boil. Simmer gently for 1-1½ hours.

The broth invariably benefits from being made one day prior to serving.

Submitted by Margaret Whitehead

Photo: Manx National Heritage

Barley Meal - Potato Bonnags

INGREDIENTS:

4oz freshly mashed Manx potatoes
6oz barley flour
1½ oz melted Manx butter
1½ teaspoons baking powder
pinch of salt
milk to mix

METHOD:

Mix together the flour, salt and baking powder. Rub in fat very thoroughly. Add potatoes and mix in lightly. Knead to a soft dough with cold milk. Turn on to a floured board, roll or pat out half inch thick. Cut into rounds and place on a greased baking sheet.

BAKE: 410°F, 210°C, Gas Mark 6-7.

TIME: 15 Minutes

IOM TT (or MGP) Veggie Pasties

INGREDIENTS

Ruff-Puff Pastry:
8 oz Flavo flour
5oz vegetable lard
½ teaspoon Salt
Cold water

Filling:
1 medium Onion
Small chunk of Swede
1 clove Garlic - crushed
Herb seasoning to taste
1 medium Carrot
2 medium potatoes
Finely chopped Parsley
Salt and Pepper to taste

METHOD

Mix flour and salt in basin. Cut lard into small pieces and mix with the flour, using a knife (do not rub in). Mix into stiff paste with cold water. Turn onto a floured board and roll out into narrow strip. Fold into three, turn one of the open ends towards you and roll again - repeat three times. Divide into 4 pieces (or 8, if smaller, lunch box size pasties are preferred) Roll each piece into circle shape. Chop all vegetables very small and mix in large bowl with seasoning. Fill pastry with mixture and add small knob of butter. Brush edges with water, fold over and seal by pinching with knife and thumb technique to crimp edges together. Paint with milk, transfer onto greased baking tray.

BAKE: Gas Mark 6 (425°-450°F), 220°C.

TIME: 30-40 minutes until golden brown

Photo: The Manx Experience (Paul Parker)

Submitted by Sue Robinson

MEATS, POULTRY & SAVOURIES

Photo: Jan Quillin - courtesy Radcliffe's Butchers, Castletown

Manx Chicken Quickie

INGREDIENTS:

4 Manx chicken legs
1-1½ oz lard
bouquet garni

3-4 rashers streaky Manx bacon
6oz mushrooms
1 packet quick onion sauce

METHOD:

Melt lard in frying pan and use to brown chicken legs. Place in casserole dish with washed and sliced mushrooms. Cut bacon into pieces, fry for 5 minutes then distribute over chicken. Mix sauce according to packet instructions, but add an extra 2 tbs milk. Pour mixture over all ingredients in casserole and add bouquet garni. Cover with lid.

BAKE: 350°F, 180°C, Gas Mark 3.

TIME: Approximately 35 minutes.

THE PARISHES OF THE ISLE OF MAN

AYRE
MICHAEL
GARFF
GLENFABA
MIDDLE
RUSHEN

The Manx Experience

Parish Chicken

INGREDIENTS: *(for four servings)*

4 manx chicken breasts   2lb apples
2 medium onions   ¾ pint chicken stock

METHOD:

Remove skin from chicken and dispose of excess fat. Peel and slice apples into thin strips. Chop onions. Place all ingredients in casserole dish or saucepan and cover with stock. Simmer gently until meat is tender.

TIME: Approximately 1 hour.

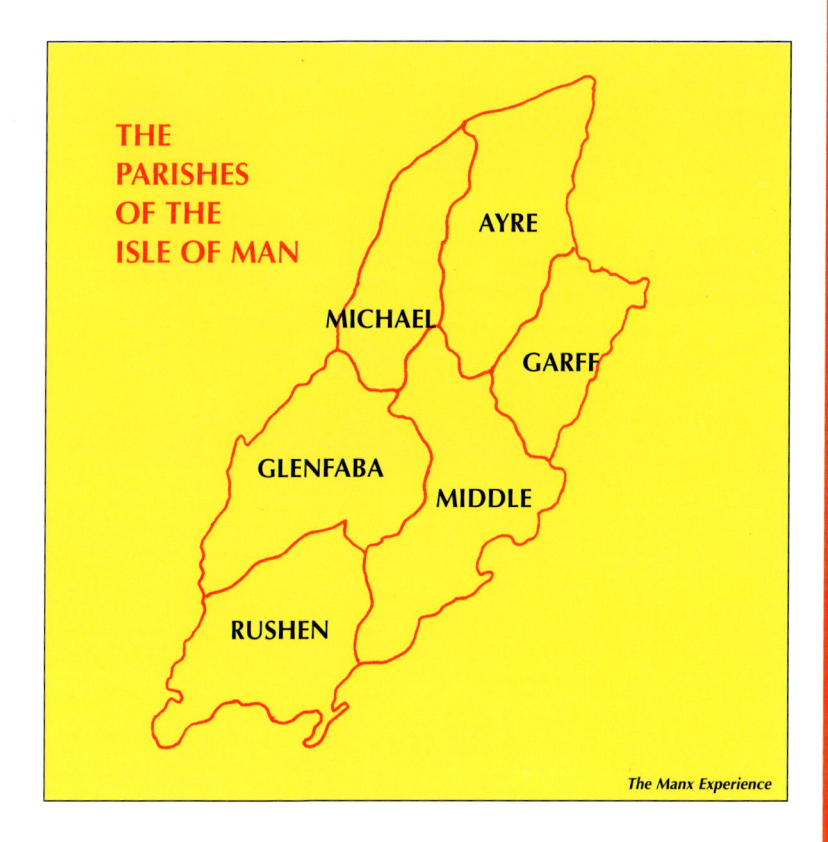

(Note: cider or Bushy's light ale may be substituted for the chicken stock.)

Submitted by Tracy Binnie (Hospice Chef)

MEATS, POULTRY & SAVOURIES

MEATS, POULTRY & SAVOURIES   Submitted by Jan Quillin

Photo: Mannin Media Group

Manx Savoury Surprise

(Vegetarian Dish)

INGREDIENTS

4 large diced Manx potatoes
4 chopped tomatoes
1 tablespoon Flavo flour
½ pint milk
salt and pepper

1 chopped onion
4 oz grated cheese
4 tablespoon chopped parsley
margarine

METHOD

Mix potatoes, onions, tomatoes, cheese, flour and parsley in a bowl and season well. Put into a dish or meat tin. Warm milk slightly and pour onto vegetables mixture. Put knobs of margarine on top.

BAKE: 400°F, 200°C, Gas Mark 6-7.

TIME: 1 hour

SERVE: Hot on its own or with meat.

Laughing Potatoes

Reminiscence – the late Paddy Lonergan (Manx Resident for over 30 years)

Photo: Jan Quillin

'When I was a boy growing up in Southern Ireland – County Tipperary, my parents used to cook what we always called – "laughing potatoes".

The potatoes were grown in our own "haggart" – (a big garden – using natural manure).

We would dig them up scrub them clean and my mother (known as Biddy) use to boil them in a huge pot that hung on a chain over a real fire.

When they were cooked they would burst open as white as snow and Father would say "they're ready now Biddy – they're laughing at us".

Then the whole family (there were 10 of us) would sit round a big wooden – white scrubbed table and the large pot was rolled down the centre of the table and we each helped ourselves with a large helping of butter and salt. With this we would have a whole pigs head at each end of the table and if the children were lucky some of them would be given a roast ear for a bit of a treat.'

Photo: Harvey Briggs

FISH & SHELLFISH

PALCHEY PHUDDASE AS SKEDDAN BYLIOOR

(Traditional Manx Greeting)

POTATOES IN PLENTY AND HERRINGS ENOUGH

Photo: Manx National Heritage

Painting: Colleen Corlett

Peel Hotpot

INGREDIENTS:

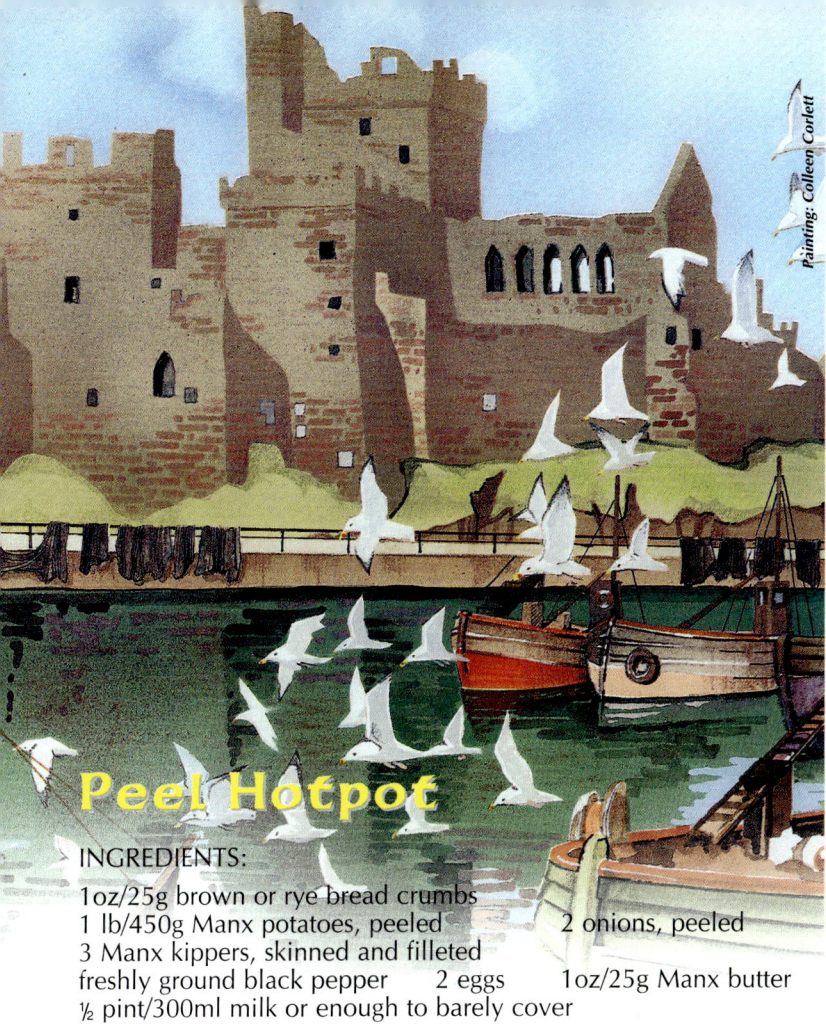

1oz/25g brown or rye bread crumbs
1 lb/450g Manx potatoes, peeled   2 onions, peeled
3 Manx kippers, skinned and filleted
freshly ground black pepper   2 eggs   1oz/25g Manx butter
½ pint/300ml milk or enough to barely cover

To garnish and serve – lemon wedges and parsley sprigs.

METHOD:

Crumble the bread into fine crumbs – set aside. Slice onions and potatoes – set aside. Butter a 750ml/1½ pint ovenproof dish and dust with the crumbs. Make layers of the potatoes, onions and kippers, seasoning the layers with pepper. Finish with a layer of potatoes, arranged in a circle. Beat the eggs and milk with a little pepper and pour over the potatoes. Dot the butter over the top.

BAKE:- Moderate oven – 350°F, 180°C, Gas mark 4.

TIME:- 30 minutes

Reduce heat to 325°F, 160°C, Gas Mark 3 for a further 30 minutes, or until the potatoes are tender. Serve hot, garnished with lemon and parsley.

FISH & SHELLFISH — Submitted by Margaret Whitehead

Photo: Jan Quiltin - Jacqui Horne, Peel

Lobster or Crab

INGREDIENTS:

1 fresh Manx lobster   sufficient salted water to cover lobster

METHOD:

Some people maintain that it's more humane to put the lobster in the freezer compartment for a few hours before cooking rather than dropping straight into boiling water.

Bring salted water to boil in fish kettle or other suitable pan. Pop in lobster. Bring back to boil for 5 minutes. Turn off heat. Remove from water. When cool enough shell. Serve.

N.B The shells can be boiled up to make a delicious fish stock.

Queenies Manx-style

INGREDIENTS

1 lb Manx Queen scallops
5 rashers Manx back bacon (diced)
small bunch fresh parsley, chopped
4 cloves fresh garlic (from bulb)
olive oil and Manx butter
1 small-diced onion

METHOD

Heat frying pan and add a dash of olive oil. Add a tablespoon of butter. Add diced bacon and onion. Fry until cooked. Add tablespoon chopped parsley and chopped cloves of garlic. Fry for approximately 1 minute. Add Queenies, approximately 2 minutes (do not over cook). Add a dash of wine and serve.

Serves 4.

Photo: Ian Quillin

FISH & SHELLFISH — *Submitted by Tracy Binnie (Hospice Chef)*

Hot Salmon Souffle

INGREDIENTS:
1 tin salmon   1 pint milk
salt & pepper   2 eggs
3oz margarine or Manx butter
3oz Flavo plain flour
good pinch of mace

deep oven proof dish (ungreased) to hold 2 pints of liquid

METHOD:
Remove any bones and break up fish with fork. Melt butter in pan, take off the heat and stir in flour. Add all milk and stir sauce over gentle heat until thickens and comes to the boil. Take pan off heat and stir in salmon. Separate yolks from whites of egg and stir yolks into mixture. Season carefully with salt, pepper and mace. Whip egg whites stiffly and fold into mixture and turn into dish.

BAKE: 380°F, 195°C, Gas mark 5.

TIME: 40 minutes

Serves 4

Photo: Jan Quillin

Submitted by Jean Walters

MANX FISH PRODUCERS ORGANISATION LIMITED

With fish becoming even more important in today's dietary conscious environment, locally sourced catches are more sought after than ever. The Manx Fish Producers Organisation Limited play a large part in the liaison of producers and fishermen and ensure that there is a quantity of locally caught fish available to the Isle of Man population.

The Organisation is pleased to support the publication of this recipe book for Hospice.

Savoury Salmon Loaf

INGREDIENTS:
½ cup buttered breadcrumbs
2 eggs slightly beaten
½ cup milk
1 lb can salmon-flaked
1 teaspoon lemon juice
½ teaspoon salt
½ teaspoon sage
pepper to taste
2 tablespoons finely chopped onion
1 tablespoon finely chopped parsley
1 tablespoon melted Manx butter

METHOD: Combine ingredients in order given. Pack firmly into buttered loaf tin.

BAKE: 350°F, 180°C, Gas Mark 4. Turn out onto platter and garnish as required

Serves 6.

Manx Fish Pie

INGREDIENTS:
about ¾lb cooked fish   1½ pint of milk   1½ oz Flavo plain flour
1 egg   breadcrumbs   1½ oz Manx butter or margarine
1 teaspoon each of sugar, salt, pepper

METHOD:
Melt fat in saucepan, remove from heat and stir in flour, add milk gradually and boil gently for 4 or 5 minutes stirring all the time. Cool slightly, stir in the fish (flaked finely with a fork) and all other ingredients – lastly beaten yolk of egg. Fold in white of egg last – beaten stiffly. Put breadcrumbs on top.

BAKE: 350°F, 180°C, Gas Mark 5-6.

TIME: ½ - ¾ hour, until brown, in well-greased pie or souffle dish. Serve with cut lemon or either prawn or mushroom sauce.

N.B: I add 1 or 2 hard-boiled eggs halved, to mixture before folding in egg white.

Manx

Grilled

1 or 2 Manx kippers
  per person
Manx Butter

Line grill rack with foil and pre-heat. Dot fleshy side of each kipper with butter and grill for about five minutes.

Poached

1 or 2 Manx kippers
  per person
Knob of Manx butter
Water

Place kippers in deep frying pan, cover with water. Add butter, cover and poach for approx 5 minutes.

Submitted by PQ, PSM.

FISH & SHELLFISH

Photo: Jan Quillin

Background photo: The Manx Experience

Kippers

Kipper Pate

1 Manx kipper cooked
1 onion
1 clove garlic
1 oz Manx butter
1 egg
4 tbls sour cream
Seasoning to taste

Boil the egg, grate and put aside. Crush garlic, finely chop onion and place both aside.

Remove skin and bones from kipper and mash the fish. Fry the onion and garlic in the butter, add to the mashed kipper, mix in egg and soured cream and season to taste.

Place into small dish and chill.

Garnish with slices of tomato and cucumber and serve with hot toast or crusty bread.

Photo: Manx National Heritage

FISH & SHELLFISH *Submitted by Mary Linehan.*

Spuds & Herring

INGREDIENTS

Salt Manx herrings   Manx potatoes
Raw Onion   1 glass buttermilk

METHOD: Soak salt herring in water overnight. Scrub potatoes, place in a large saucepan and barely cover with water. When the potatoes are past the half-cooked stage, lay herring on top in saucepan. When both potatoes and herring are cooked remove herring carefully, drain potatoes and serve with slices of raw onion and knobs of butter.
This is a traditional dish and should be accompanied by a glass of buttermilk.

Photo: Manx National Heritage

Cider Haddock Casserole

INGREDIENTS:

1 lb haddock
2 sliced tomatoes
¼ pint cider
2 table spoons fresh White & Healthy breadcrumbs
2oz mushrooms
1 table spoon chopped parsley
1 table spoon grated cheese

METHOD:

Skin, bone and cut fish into cubes place in a casserole dish, add mushrooms, tomatoes, seasoning and parsley. Pour cider over ingredients, cover with foil.

BAKE: 350°F, 180°C, Gas Mark 4.

TIME: 35-40 minutes

When cooked top with cheese and breadcrumbs. Brown under grill.

FISH & SHELLFISH Submitted by Sue Robinson

29

" Fishermen tell a lot of tales about the size of fish they catch "

Tom Cregeen (Castletown)

T he importance of agriculture and fishing to the future of the Isle of Man has always been paramount and continues to be so to the present time.

The **Manx National Farmers Union** plays a significant part in the agricultural community through its recognition of farmers' interests and its desire to ensure that the produce of its members is recognised as being of the highest quality. Similarly, the contribution of the Island's **Young Farmers** through their expertise and their enthusiasm consolidates and assists in securing the future of the industry at a time when investment in the future is a matter of significant importance.

Manx Fish Producers Organisation Limited looks after the interests of the Island's fishermen who, though now much reduced in numbers, still ensure that locally-caught fish remains of the highest standard.

All three organisations are pleased to be associated with this book, which will assist Hospice.

Photo: Jan Quillin

*We may live without poetry, music and art,
We may live without conscience and live without heart,
We may live without friends,
We may live without books,
But civilized man cannot live without cooks.*

*He may live without books – what is knowledge but grieving
He may live without hope – what is hope but deceiving,
He may live without love – what is passion but pining,
But where is the man who can live without dining.*

*Owen Meridith
1831-1891*

Ramsey Bakery

CAKES

St Bridget's Delight

Photo: Jan Quillin

INGREDIENTS

Scone Mix -

1 lb Sunrise self raising flour
½ level teaspoon salt
4oz Manx butter
2oz sugar
about ½ pint milk

500g block marzipan
3 tins (400g size) pears halves
heaped tablespoon brown sugar
heaped tablespoon cinnamon

METHOD:

Make scone mix. Roll out about 1 inch thick onto a tray or 8 inch round tins. Top with pear halves. Sprinkle with brown sugar. Grate block of Marzipan over top. Sprinkle with cinnamon.

BAKE: 425°F, 220°C, Gas Mark 7.

TIME: Approx 12-15min until golden brown. Serve hot with cream or custard.

Weetabix Cakes

LAXEY GLEN MILLS LTD.

INGREDIENTS:

3 Weetabix   ½ lb dark brown sugar   1 egg
6oz dried fruit   ½ pint milk
7½ oz Sunrise self-raising flour

METHOD: Soak all ingredients (except flour and egg) overnight. Sieve flour, add to mixture and egg. Beat all ingredients together. Put into 2lb loaf tin.

BAKE: 350°F, 180°C, Gas Mark 4.

TIME: 1 Hour

Photo: The Manx Experience

Submitted by Marjorie Harper

Lemon Apple Pie

INGREDIENTS:

3oz sugar   2oz margarine
4oz grated apple   1 egg
2 tablespoons (approx.) lemon juice and a little grated lemon rind.
6" pastry case

METHOD:

Line flan dish or flan ring with pastry. Cream margarine, sugar and lemon rind. Add beaten egg. Add grated apple and lemon juice and mix well (it may have a curdled appearance but do not worry, that is all right). Pour into pastry case.

BAKE: 350°F, 180°C, Gas Mark 5.

TIME: 30-40 Minutes.

Moist Guinness Cake

INGREDIENTS:

500gms Flavo flour
250gms brown or white sugar
2tsps mixed spice
1kg sultanas or raisins or 500gms each
½ bottle Guinness (original)

250gms Manx butter
1 tsp baking powder
3 eggs

METHOD: Rub fat into flour (or process), add sugar, spices and baking powder. Add dried fruit and mix well. Add beaten eggs and Guinness to make a soft mixture.

BAKE: 270°F, 120°/130°C, Gas Mark 1.

TIME: 3-3½ hours. Test with skewer - cake is cooled when skewer emerges clean.

Manx National Heritage

CAKES *Submitted by Lyndsay Wilkinson*

Rich Fruit Cake

INGREDIENTS:

450g (1 lb) currants
175g (6oz) sultanas
175g raisins
50g (2oz) glace cherries
50g mixed peel finely chopped
3 tablespoons brandy
225g (8oz) Flavo plain flour
½ teaspoon salt
¼ teaspoon grated nutmeg

½ teaspoon full mixed spice
225g unsalted Manx butter
225g soft brown sugar
4 large eggs
50g chopped almonds
1 dessertspoon black treacle
grated rind of 1 lemon
grated rind of 1 orange

PREPARATION: Preheat oven to gas mark 1 (275°F/140°C). Line 8" round cake tin with greaseproof paper. Grease tin.

METHOD: Place all dried fruit and peel in a bowl and mix in the brandy. Cover bowl and leave to soak for at least 12 hours. Sieve flour, salt and spices in a large bowl. Cream butter and sugar in another bowl until light and fluffy. Beat eggs. Add tablespoon at a time into creamed mixture, then fold in flour and spices. Stir in fruit and peel, nuts, treacle and rinds. Spoon into prepared cake tin. Smooth top. Tie band of brown paper around outside of tin. Cover cake with double square of greaseproof paper.

BAKE: 275°F, 140°C, Gas Mark 1.

TIME: 4-4¾ approximately. Do not even peek at it until 4 hours have passed. When cold, wrap in greaseproof paper. Store in air tight tin until ready to decorate.

Photo: Manx National Heritage

Submitted by Margaret Whitehead.

Cake made by Jill McBride

Mrs Blinkhorn's Apple Pie

Mrs Blinkhorn's Apple Pie was so delicious and well-liked that it inspired George Crawford of Oban, Argyll to write a tune about it.

INGREDIENTS

8oz Sunrise self raising flour
2oz lard
3lb of apples

2oz Manx butter or margarine
pinch of salt

METHOD: Prepare apples. Stew them with sugar. Leave to cool. Roll out pastry. Line 8" pie dish, add apples, brush edge with water cover with lid, flute edges of pastry and cut slit in top. Brush pastry with milk and sprinkle with sugar.

BAKE: 375°F, 190°C, Gas Mark 4.

TIME: 30 minutes.

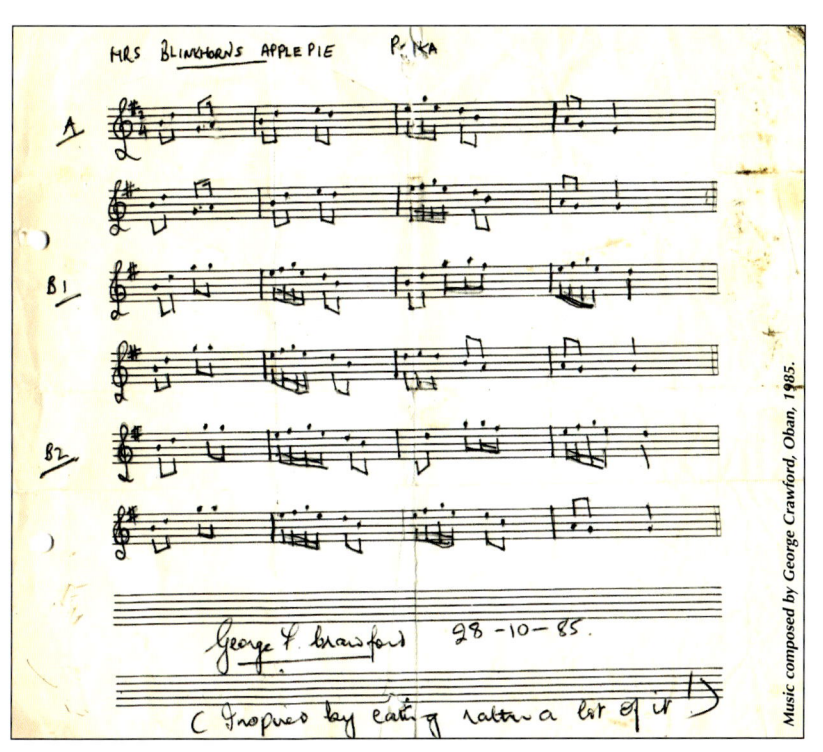

Music composed by George Crawford, Oban, 1985.

CAKES — *Submitted by Jan Quillin (Mrs Blinkhorn's daughter)*

Mother's Spiced Rock Cakes

INGREDIENTS

4oz Manx butter or margarine
pinch of salt
4oz currants
½ teaspoon cinnamon or mixed spice
a little milk
8oz Sunrise self raising flour
4oz castor sugar
1 egg, beaten

METHOD: Sieve flour, spice and salt in a mixing bowl. Add margarine/butter. Rub in to flour until like breadcrumbs. Mix in fruit, sugar and eggs to a firm paste. Fork small heaps of mixture onto greased baking tray.

BAKE: 350°F, 180°C, Gas Mark 4.

TIME: 20 minutes/or until lightly browned.

Plum Slices

INGREDIENTS

1lb plums (alternatively, apples, apricots, dates prunes or leftover mincemeat)
Teaspoon cinnamon
5oz porridge oats
8oz Manx butter
10oz Manx Queen bread flour
teaspoon salt
4oz sugar

METHOD

Melt butter and sugar in a saucepan. Cut up plums, remove stones and cover with cinnamon. Grease a 10" x 6" x 1" baking tin. Pour melted mixture onto dry ingredients and mix well until all ingredients are well-coated. With half of mixture, cover base of baking tin, add a layer of plums and cover with remaining mixture.

BAKE: 400°F, 200°C, Gas Mark 6.

TIME: 25 minutes.

Allow to cool for 10 minutes then slice into 15 pieces. Leave to cool further on wire tray.

Luscious Lemon Cake

INGREDIENTS:

100g (4oz) Manx butter or soft margarine 175g (6oz) caster sugar
175g (6oz) Sunrise sifted self-raising flour 2 large eggs
finely grated rind of one lemon 4 tablespoons of milk

For the Syrup:
3 rounded tablespoon sifted icing or granulated sugar
juice of 1 lemon

METHOD: Line and grease 900g. loaf tin. Cream butter and sugar. Add eggs, flour, lemon rind and milk. Mix well to a soft dropping consistency. Put into tin and smooth the top.

BAKE: Preheat at 350°F, 180°C, Gas Mark 4.

TIME: Bake for 40-45 minutes until firm.

Mix syrup mixture (cold) and pour over cake as soon as it comes out of oven. Leave in tin until completely cold before turning out.

Submitted by Mary Edge

Photo: Jan Quillin

Photo: Jan Quillin

Easter Simnel Cake

INGREDIENTS:

6oz Manx butter or margarine
10oz mixed fruit
2oz glace cherries
6oz Flavo plain flour
3 teaspoons mixed spice
250gm packet of almond paste

3 eggs
6oz brown sugar - soft
2 tablespoons milk
1 teaspoon baking powder
grated rind of orange

PREPARATION: Grease and line 7" baking tin. Place half of the mixture in the baking tin then add 1 cube of almond paste and cover with remaining mixture.

METHOD: Cream butter and sugar. Add eggs. Add dry ingredients. Add orange rind and milk.

BAKE: 325°F, 160°C, Gas Mark 2.

TIME: 2½ hours approx.

When cooked roll out almond paste and cover top of cake, then roll 11 almond balls and place along the edge of the cake and, if desired, add other Easter decorations.

Submitted by Mary Edge

Christmas Cake

INGREDIENTS

METRIC	IMPERIAL
175g currants	6oz currants
225g stoned raisins, chopped	8oz stoned raisins, chopped
225g sultanas	8oz sultanas
100g glace cherries, halved	4oz glace cherries, halved
100g mixed peel	4oz mixed peel
50g angelica, chopped	2oz angelica, chopped
50g chopped almonds	2oz chopped almonds
Finely grated rind of 1 lemon	Finely grated rind of 1 lemon
225g Flavo plain flour	8oz Flavo plain flour
1 5ml spoon mixed spice	1 teaspoon of mixed spice
225g Manx butter, softened	8oz Manx butter, softened
225g soft brown sugar	8oz soft brown sugar
1 15ml spoon black treacle	1 tablespoon black treacle
4 large eggs	4 large eggs
1-2 15ml spoons brandy or sherry	1-2 tablespoons brandy or sherry

METHOD:
Grease and line a 20cm (8in) round cake tin. Tie newspaper or brown paper band around the tin. Put all the dried fruit in a bowl. Stir in the nuts and lemon rind. Sieve the flour and spice together. Cream the butter, sugar and treacle together until light and fluffy. Beat in the eggs, stir in the sieved flour and spices. Finally stir in the mixed fruit and mix thoroughly. Turn into the tin and make a slight hollow in the centre.

BAKE: In a slow oven 300°F, 150°C, Gas Mark 2.

TIME: 3½ - 4 hours. Cool in the tin before turning out on a wire rack to cool completely. Prick the surface of the cake all over with a fine skewer and pour over brandy or sherry before storing.

TO ICE: Almond paste the cake first using 675g (1½ lb) ready-made almond paste. Allow a few days for this to harden before applying the icing. Make royal icing using 3 egg whites and ¾kg (1½ lb) icing sugar and 2 x 5ml spoons (2 teaspoons) glycerine. Rough ice the cake and use bought decorations to decorate.

Photo: Manx National Heritage

Submitted by Peggy Foster

Manx Sweet Pancakes

INGREDIENTS:

6oz Flavo plain flour
¾ level teaspoon bicarbonate of soda
½ level teaspoon cream of tartar
1 tablespoon caster sugar

pinch of salt
1 large egg
¼ pint of milk

METHOD:

Mix altogether into a batter. Cook on griddle – heat enough oil to cover surface. Test batter when ready. Drop tablespoon amounts and cook until brown. Turn and repeat.

Serve with butter, jam and cream (optional)

Photo: Manx National Heritage

CAKES *Submitted by Mary Edge*

43

"After 63 years,
I still get a 'buzz' when
my cakes come out
of the oven."

Mary Edge
(St Bridget's Day Unit - 2003)

Photo: Manx National Heritage

". . . crusty, homebaked bread,
with the mealy savour of ripe wheat
roundly in your mouth and under your teeth,
roasted sweet and crisp and deep brown . . ."

Richard Llewellyn
Author - *How Green was My Valley*

FRESH BREAD DELIVERED EVERY DAY

For the last 33 years, at the crack of dawn a fleet of Ramsey Bakery vans sets out to service every store in the Island, from corner shop to supermarket, with bread baked during the previous night - truly a local service.

Ramsey Bakery have pleasure in supporting the production of "The Manx Kitchen" for Hospice.

RAMSEY BAKERY LIMITED
Station Road : Ramsey : Isle of Man
Telephone 01624 813624 : Fax 01624 816221

BREADS, BUN LOAVES & PUDDINGS

45

Ginger Bread

INGREDIENTS:

4 level tablespoons of syrup
3 oz Flavo plain flour
1 level teaspoon bicarbonate of soda
1½ oz porridge oats
2 level teaspoons ground ginger
¼ pint of milk   3oz Manx butter
1 egg

METHOD:

Melt the butter, sugar and syrup over a low heat. Mix in the remaining ingredients and place in an 8" square cake tin.

BAKE: 325°F, 160°C, Gas Mark 3.

TIME: 45 Minutes.

Photo: Manx National Heritage

Meg's Manx Bonnag

INGREDIENTS:

2.5 cups Flavo plain flour
1 cup currants
1 large teaspoon mixed spice
1 teaspoon bicarbonate of soda

1 cup sugar
1 cup butter milk
1 tablespoon butter
1 dash vanilla essence

METHOD:

Mix the dry ingredients. Rub in butter gradually. Add buttermilk and vanilla essence. Mix to a smooth dough, adding more liquid if needed. Form into a round

BAKE: 350°F, 180°C, Gas Mark 4.

TIME: 1 hour

Submitted by Tracy Binnie

BREADS, BUN LOAVES & PUDDINGS

Vitamin Loaf

(No knead bread inspired by Doris Grant)

INGREDIENTS

1½ lbs Laxey Glen Mills Wholemeal flour
1 lb white organic flour   2oz seasame seeds
2oz pumpkin seeds   2oz sunflower seeds
1oz brewers yeast   1oz quinoa flakes
2 packets of dried yeast   1½ litres of lukewarm water
3 tablespoons honey or black molasses or mixture
tablespoon poppy seeds (to sprinkle on top of loaf)

METHOD: Grease 3 x 2lb loaf tins and put in oven to warm. Warm all utensils and bowl. Dry ingredients. Mix molasses/honey with luke-warm water, then add to mixture. Stir thoroughly until dough feels elastic and leaves sides of the bowl clean. Divide the dough, which should be slippery but not wet between 3 loaf tins.

THE RISING: Cover tins with a cloth and put in a warm place for about 20 minutes or until the dough is within a half inch from the top of the tins.

BAKE: In pre heated oven – 400°F, 200°C, Gas Mark 6.

TIME: 35-40 minutes

Turn out of tins and leave to cool on wire tray. Delicious toasted!

Photo: Harvey Briggs

Date and Walnut Loaf

INGREDIENTS:

8oz Sunrise self raising flour
3oz margarine/Manx butter
1 egg dropped in ½ cup milk

4oz caster sugar
4oz date and walnuts

METHOD: Mix all dry ingredients. Add fruit, egg and milk.

BAKE: 325°F, 160°C, Gas Mark 2.

TIME: 1 hour.

Bushy's Ale Buns

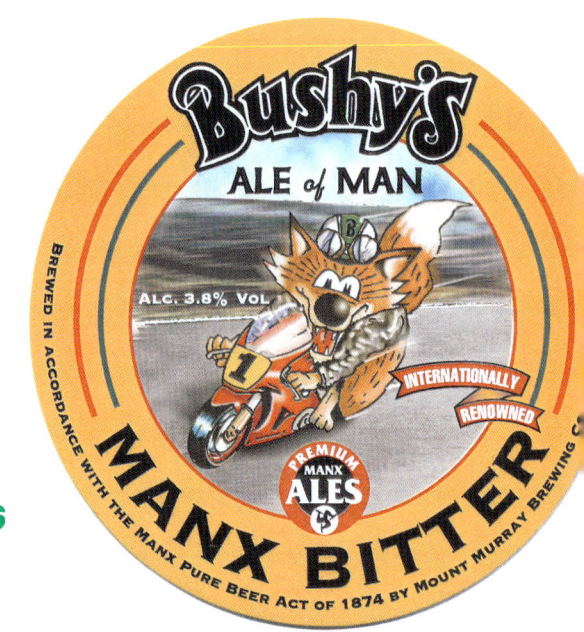

Submitted by Sue Robinson.

Beer Mat courtesy Bushy's Ale of Man

INGREDIENTS:

1lb Laxey Glen Mills wholemeal flour
8oz Flavo flour
¾ pint Bushy's Brown Ale
1oz fresh yeast or dried packet yeast
2 level teaspoons salt
2 tbs vegetable oil

METHOD:

Yeast starter: dissolve yeast in tablespoons of the Bushy's Ale and leave in a warm place until frothy.
The mix: bring remaining ale and the oil to the boil, then allow to cool to lukewarm. Mix the flours and salt in a large mixing bowl. Add the warm ale and the yeast mixture and make dough. Knead for about 10 minutes until smooth.
First rising: cover and leave to rise in a warm place until double its original size.
Second rising: knead for a further 2-3 minutes. Shape into 12 balls and place with the sides touching, in a greased roasting tin. Cover and leave to rise a second time for approximately 30-35 minutes until double in size.

BAKE: In a pre-heated oven - 400°F, 200°C, Gas Mark 6.

TIME: 35 minutes.

Cool and break apart into small buns.

Soda Wheaten

INGREDIENTS:

1lb (450g) Laxey Glen Mills wholemeal flour
½lb (225g) Flavo plain flour   ¾ pint sour milk   2 teaspoons salt
2 teaspoons bicarbonate of soda

METHOD:

Mix the wholemeal flour with white flour, adding the salt and the soda. Make a well in the centre of the mix and pour in the milk continuing to mix with a wooden spoon. Knead dough into ball with floured hands. Turn onto a floured board, flatten by hand into a circle approximately 1½" thick. Take a floured knife and mark a cross on the top so that it can be easily broken into quarters when baked.

BAKE: 425°F, 220°C, Gas Mark 7 then reduce to 350°F, 180°C, Gas Mark 4.

TIME: 25 minutes then 15 minutes at lower temperature.

This bread should not be cut until 6 hours after it is removed from the oven. *(Note: Buttermilk or fresh milk may be used instead of sour milk.)*

Photo: Jan Quillin

Submitted by Peg Floyd.

Oatmeal Bread

INGREDIENTS:

9oz (350g) Laxey Glen Mills Wholemeal flour   1 tbs vegetable oil
½ pint (300ml) warm milk   3oz (120g) Flavo plain flour
2 level teaspoons salt   8oz (250g) rolled oats or medium oatmeal

Yeast starter: 2 teaspoons dried yeast   ¼ pint (150ml) warm water
                1 teaspoon honey

Preparation: Pour the warm milk over the rolled oats/oatmeal and leave for 30 minutes.
Yeast Starter: Dissolve the honey in warm water, sprinkle dried yeast on top and set aside for about 10 minutes until frothy.

METHOD:

Mix together the flour and salt in a bowl, add the oil, yeast liquid and oat mixture. Mix well, turn onto a floured board and knead for 10 minutes.
First rising: wash the bowl, then oil it and replace the dough. Cover with oiled polythene and leave to rise in a warm place until double in size (approximately 1 hour).
Second rising: knead the dough again for about 3 minutes. Divide into 2 pieces and shape into loaves. Place in 2 well-greased 1lb (500g) bread tins. Cover with oiled polythene and leave to rise again in a warm place for about 40 minutes.

BAKE: 400°F, 200°C, Gas Mark 6.

TIME: 30 minutes. Cool on a rack.

Photo: Laxey Glen Mills

Submitted by Pam Fuller.

Manx Bunloaf

INGREDIENTS:

½ lb Laxey Glen Mills Soda Bread flour
2oz caster sugar
¼ lb sultanas
¼ lb margarine
¼ pint buttermilk
1 egg

METHOD:

Rub margarine well into flour. Add sugar to the flour. Add sultanas. Beat egg and add milk and egg to mixture.

BAKE: 350°F, 180°C, Gas Mark 4.

TIME: 1 hour

Photo: Jan Quillin

Manx Bramble Mousse

INGREDIENTS:

1lb blackberries
4ozs caster sugar
2 tbs water
whipped Manx cream to taste

3 Manx eggs
½oz gelatine
juice of ½ lemon

METHOD:

Check all the fresh fruit and remove any foreign 'bodies'. Place into saucepan along with a tablespoon of the sugar and heat gently stirring constantly, until fruit is soft. Pass through a strainer to remove pips and allow to cool. Immerse gelatine into the lemon juice and water to soak. Beat the eggs and the remainder of the sugar together until the mixture is creamy and stiff. Melt the gelatine over a low heat, fold into egg mixture, followed by half of the blackberries added in the same manner. Finally add in a portion of the whipped cream. Pour completed mixture into a glass bowl and allow to set in refrigerator for several hours. When serving add some of the remaining blackberries along with the whipped cream.

Photo: The Manx Experience - Colin Slack

Photo: The Manx Experience

Cold Deemster Sweet

INGREDIENTS (for 6 servings):

¾ bitter chocolate
3 ½ oz crushed digestive biscuits
3 ½ oz icing sugar
3 teaspoons cold water
2oz peeled grapes

3 ½ oz Manx butter
4 teaspoons dry sherry
3 teaspoons Manx double cream
2 eggs
2oz chopped nuts

METHOD:

Soften chocolate with water and beat well. Beat in butter and place in mixing bowl. Beat in yolks of eggs and stir in sugar, Add stiffly beaten egg whites, peeled grapes, chopped nuts, crushed biscuits and sherry. Combine all in mixer, then place in buttered cake tin and freeze. Remove from tin ½ hour before serving and decorate according to taste. This sweet can be kept frozen for up to a week.

Submitted by Mary Linehan.

Manx Pudding

4 oz Flavo plain flour
2 eggs
1 oz currants
Pinch salt
½ pt milk

Sieve the flour and salt and make a well in the centre. Add the eggs and mix in the flour gradually, slowly adding the milk. Beat well until the mixture is full of bubbles. Stir in the currants. Pour into a greased pudding basin. Cover and steam for about two hours.

Serve with creamy custard.

Photo: Manx National Heritage

Gaelic Coffee Trifle

INGREDIENTS
1 packet trifle sponges
30ml (2 tbsp) coffee essence (e.g. 'Camp')
568ml (1 pt) milk
25g (1oz) Manx (or Irish) butter
Walnut halves to decorate
60ml (4 tbsp) Manx spirit
75g (3ozs) caster sugar
75g (3ozs) cornflour
2 egg yolks
300ml (10fl oz) fresh Manx double cream

METHOD:
Place trifle sponges into glass bowl. Mix half of the coffee essence (15ml) with 45ml (3 tbsp) of the Manx whisky and pour over sponges. Place the sugar, cornflour and milk in a saucepan. Heat, stirring continuously until sauce thickens and boils. Cook gently for 3 minutes. Remove from heat and stir in the egg yolks and remaining coffee. Cook for a further minute, remove from heat and mix in remaining butter and whisky. Cool.
Whip the fresh cream until softly stiff. Fold half the fresh cream into the coffee mixture. Spoon over the trifle sponges. Decorate with remaining fresh cream and walnuts.

Serves six.

Submitted by Mary Linehan

Baked Rice Pudding Manx-style

INGREDIENTS:

1½ oz rice
1oz sugar
Grated nutmeg/cinnamon
knob Manx butter
1 pint milk
pinch of salt

METHOD:

Wash rice. Place rice, butter, sugar, milk and salt into greased fire-proof dish and grate nutmeg or sprinkle cinnamon on top. Bake until creamy, stirring once or twice during the first hour.

BAKE: Middle shelf - 300°F, 150°C, Gas Mark 2.

TIME: 3 hours.

Serves 3-4 people. The recipe is improved by the addition, when serving, of a large tablespoonful of Davison's Manx Ice Cream.

Rice Pudding

Mill days were great social occasions, with the better-run farms serving the best of traditional food and always providing a large rice pudding over which everyone fought for the 'skin'.

One threshing day, on a farm in Santon, when the big enamel bowl of rice pudding was placed on the table . . .

"Here's your helping, Arty," said the lady of the farm, - in jest.

"Good," said Arty, and ate the lot - in earnest!

Well-known Manx story.

Photo: Capt. Stephen Carter

*For rabbits hot and rabbits cold,
For rabbits young and rabbits old,
For rabbits tender and rabbits tough,
I thank the Lord, I've had enough.*

Unknown

The Gibb family who farmed on the Calf of Man 100 years ago used this prayer at meal times.

Photo: Jan Quillin

Manx Honey Fudge

INGREDIENTS

2 cups sugar
 teaspoon salt
 cup Manx honey

2 oz plain chocolate
Cup evaporated milk
2 tablespoons Manx butter

Boil sugar, chocolate, salt and milk for 5 minutes. Add honey and cook until mixture can be made into a soft ball. Remove from heat and add butter. Put aside until lukewarm, then beat until creamy and pour into buttered tray. Cut into wedges when firm.

Treacle Toffee

INGREDIENTS:

8oz black treacle
2oz Manx butter

1 cup of sugar
1 tablespoon vinegar

METHOD: Melt all the ingredients together in a heavy pan. When boiling point is reached keep at rolling boil and continue stirring for 15 minutes. Take the pan from the heat. To test setting point drop a spot of the liquid into a cup of ice cold water. Transfer to a chilled Swiss roll tin and leave to set.

Photo: Jan Quillin

Victoria Plum or Damson Ketchup

INGREDIENTS (Makes 3½ pints):

8 lbs plums or damsons
1 lb onions chopped small
2ozs salt

8ozs currants
2 pints white vinegar
1 lb demerara sugar

Place the following in a piece of gauze:

6-8 dried chillies
1 tablespoon mustard seeds
2 whole garlic cloves

1 tablespoon black peppercorn
½ oz dried root ginger crushed

METHOD

Remove stones from plums. Place in a large pan. Add currants, onions and the bag of spices. Add 1 pint of the vinegar. Bring to boil. Simmer uncovered until mixture is soft - about 30 minutes. Remove spices. Place contents of pan in a liquidiser. Blend and/or sieve until smooth. Rinse pan. Return puree and bag of spices. Add salt, sugar, remaining vinegar. Simmer for 1½ -2 hours or until ketchup has reduced to 3½ pints. Stir occasionally. Prepare containers. Used ketchup bottles are ideal. Pour hot ketchup into bottles. Put on tops but screw only halfway. Place bottles in a large deep pan standing them upside down on a heat proof plate. Add warm water to within 1½ inches of the top. Bring water to the boil - after 10 minutes remove bottles from pan and complete the sealing.

The Late Margaret Whitehead - stalwart of St Bridget's

Manx Blackberry Wine

INGREDIENTS:

3lb blackberries
Sugar
Brandy

METHOD:

Place blackberries in stone jar with three dessert spoonfuls of sugar. Leave for three weeks, stirring each day. Strain through muslin bag and add one pound of sugar to each pint of blackberry juice. Pour into bottles, adding one dessert spoonful of brandy to each bottle. Cork and leave for a few weeks to age.

Fudge

INGREDIENTS:

2oz Manx butter
large tin sweetened condensed milk
1lb sugar
4tbs water

METHOD:

Place sugar, butter and water into a large saucepan. Stir gently until the sugar is dissolved. Add condensed milk and bring to the boil. Simmer on a very low heat for approximately 30 minutes until the mixture thickens and browns. Stir occasionally as it simmers. Remove from heat and beat thoroughly. Pour into greased tray and wait until it is completely set. Cut into squares and serve.

Manx Choco Pots

INGREDIENTS:

6oz plain chocolate
2 tbs cream
3 eggs

METHOD:

For the chocolate, you may either grate a bar of chocolate or use the powdered type.

Separate egg whites and yolks and whip the whites stiffly. Melt the chocolate in a *bain-marie* or use a bowl in a saucepan of hot water on the stove. Remove bowl from heat, beat in the egg yolks, fold in the whites, turn into ramekins or small dishes, chill and serve. You may enhance the dish with a little whipped cream on top if you wish. The dish stores for days.

* To obtain more juice from a lemon or orange – warm the fruit (whole) for seconds in a microwave or in a bowl of hot water.

* Use a wooden squeezer to gather juice.

* To stop the smell of cabbage filling the house – put a piece of greaseproof over the pan and scrunch around edges.

* The secret of good sponge recipes is to weigh the eggs – to equal the same weight as butter and add half an eggshell full of warm water.

* Don't handle pastry too much it spoils the texture.

* Use vegetable lard for pastry.

* To cut fruit cake or fresh bread always use a hot knife.

* When cake making always sift the flour.

* After covering the top of fruit cakes remember to cut a hole the size of a 50 pence piece in the centre of the greaseproof paper.

* Cover frozen garden peas with boiling water, after 5 minutes strain and serve with salad – no cooking.

* Secret of not burning butter when frying is to add olive oil.

* To test if a cake is cooked before taking it out of the oven – insert skewer for 16 seconds. Remove. If wet mixture remains on skewer return to the oven for a longer bake.

TIPS AND WRINKLES

Just some of the staff at St Bridget's.

ST BRIDGET'S HOSPICE

is part of the Hospice Care charity that provides specialist palliative care for people of the Isle of Man ensuring that such care is made available at no cost to patients and families, irrespective of race, religion, background or beliefs.

Palliative care means holistic care provided by a multi-professional team for those whose disease may no longer be curable. It enables them to achieve the best possible quality of life during the final stages of their illness that may take weeks or months. The majority of the cost is funded by fundraising activities and legacies. Some Government funding is also made available.

Our team at St Bridget's works well together and strives to achieve one aim - to provide physical, emotional, social and spiritual care to those who need it.

The multi-professional team consists of:
10-bed In-patient Unit : Doctors : Day Therapy Unit
Community Specialist Nurses (Macmillan nurses) : Lymphoedema Service
Hospital Specialist Nurses : Occupational Therapy : Physiotherapy
Social Worker : Bereavement Counselling Service : Complementary Therapy

Hospice Care could not deliver the service without the hard work and commitment of our many volunteers. As the hospice continues its enormous expansion of the last 21 years, we hope to continue to build on the excellence in care we have developed, and extend our services in the new hospice that is planned for the very near future which will also include a children's facility.

St Bridget's Hospice is indebted to every person and organisation who has assisted in the production of "The Manx Kitchen".